Why is a spy called a MOLE?

Commander George Washington and Christopher McMole

BOOK 5

Written and Illustrated by
Lorraine Strieby

LORRAINE STRIEBY was awarded the Sandro Botticelli Prize that was given to her on March 1st, 2015, inside the Museum Home of Dante Alighieri in Florence, Italy.

She was selected for this honor by Mr. Paolo Levi, director of the "Eetto Arte Magazine," and given a full page displaying her art.

She also has been selected as one of 50 artists who participated in La Grande Exposition Universelle in Paris, the Eiffel Tower, to show her painting, Clarinet Blues in the Wunderkammer "The Secret Room of Art" Palermo Museum, Sicily, by Mr. Francesco Saverio Russo, international art consultant.

Three of her painting are on permanent display in the Southern Nevada Museum of Fine Art, Las Vegas, Nevada. Represented by the Amsterdam, Whitney Gallery, New York. Artist of UNICEF Woman of the Year, Women's Radio Network, New York 2015.

Original Concept Artist, Tournament of Roses Parade Float, sponsored by West Virginia University, Children's Hospital and Children's Miracle Network. Float Name: "Wild & Wonderful".

DEDICATED TO

All my family who have given me their love and support,
to my grandchildren: Stephanie, Dylan, Michelle, and Marc.
To Vicki, Lisa, Lori, Ann, Mike, and Stan.
To all the people that have believed in this project,
to my graphic designers at CRS Design Center:
Monica R. Garcia and Carlos Rodas,
and to all who are young at heart.

Also creator of WannaBTruckers, a travel game sold in Amazon.
www.wannaBTruckersboardgame.com • www.LorraineStrieby.com
First e-book edition 2014

Foreword

This book was born because I had finished the Adventures of Mayor Molly McMole and her ancestor, Christopher, just popped in to my head with firm persistence.

Then too, after reading Ron Chernow's, *Washington A Life*, he confirmed that he was a true hero and our country was divinely inspired. Our founding fathers are often overlooked in our schools today along with the hero, Mr. Billy Lee, unfortunately he was profoundly overlooked!

As it often happens, top spies never meet their leader and that was the case with Christopher. The storytellers probably will learn some facts while reading to the little ones. This is a whimsical book based on fact.

The British were destined to fail right away because they fought in Appalachia and Commander Washington was a surveyor at the age of 15, and explored Virginia clear to the Ohio River. He fought with his men and learned fighting techniques from the American Indians.

At first I was not going to write much about Benjamin Franklin, but realized a "no can do" when I discovered that he was responsible for the French supplying a 24 ship armada led by a brilliant admiral that helped destroy the British at Yorktown, Virginia.

One thing I have never been able to figure out is why France is not our mother country. Since others have claimed otherwise, France is the best stepmother we could have had.

One more thing, the human spy, Mr. John André, was caught on a lonely road at night by low-ranking American soldiers, saving the lives of Washington, Hamilton, and Mr. Billy Lee. They found the plans in his sock.

While going through my mail one day, I found a picture of a painting by Henri Rousseau and there in the *Surprised!* painting were Andre's boots. See if you can find them. Thank you, Henri, I was certainly surprised, and thank you for reading my book--a Washington love story. You will probably be surprised, too.
Lorraine Strieby

Dear Reader,
How many owls can you find in this book?
Thanks for reading this book and looking
for the owls.
Lorraine Strieby

PROLOGUE

Major George Washington
At age twenty-one
Rafts up the Monongahela River
Around Morgantown, Virginia
(Now Morgantown, West Virginia).
He and his troops are going to help
Win the French-Indian War.
For him it is an amazing debut.
The British take notice
Of his fighting skills.
They hardly know
What he is going to put them through
Get ready, King George III.
Another George is here.

Big question--
Have you ever wondered why a spy is
called a mole?
Well, here is the reason why:

One stormy night
Near Halloween,
When things were not right.
Quite scary in fact,
Commander George Washington,
Mr. Billy Lee, and Lieutenant Colonel
Alexander Hamilton
Were on their way to Fort West Point
On the Hudson River
To check on the Fort's Strength.

The winds were blowing,
About 40 knots
And they could go no further.
They stayed at a friend's house
So they could eat and slumber
Even though it started to thunder.

Before going to bed
The horses and Madam Moose
had to be watered and fed.
Nelson, Washington's horse,
A celebrity in his own right,
And the General's favorite dog,
A dalmatian, named Madam Moose,
Who guarded the horses
From wild wolves who were on the loose.
She sensed there was a wolf near by.

The next morning they thanked their host.
The weather was clear
And shortly they were there,
At West Point!

Yikes, no one was there to meet and greet!
The great Commander
And his aide, Hamilton,
were used to protocol.
Washington was alarmed.
Where was Benedict Arnold?
He was the boss of this place.
Washington wasn't used to being stood up!

Near the gate they met Corporal Roeby
Who had a U.S. Army dog named Toby,
a blind wolf-dog, U.S.W.D.-01
With a sensational sense of smell and
Could hear a wolf's howl
as far away as 10 nauticals

Washington waited one hour,
Pacing back and forth.
Roeby gave Wolf Dog Arnold's
Blue Jacket that was left behind.

Toby took a big whiff,
Everyone followed Wolf Dog
Down to the Hudson River that was
running swift.
Arnold's barge was gone.
Arnold was gone!

While wary Washington and
Horrified Hamilton
were galloping on their horses,
Following Arnold's barge downstream,
On the hill with his tiny spyglass
Was Christopher McMole,
U.S. Spy No. M-01, and
His aide, Wolf Dog WD-14.

McMole saw the worst!!!
Traitor Benedict Arnold was boarding
The H.M.S. Vulture--a ghastly ship
With three masts.
McMole gasped, and Wolf Dog Howled
Alerting WD-15.

Christopher wanted to know
What Arnold was up to.
Strange that his crew
of three went up the ladder first.
Then the deceitful
Benedict Arnold--now at large,
Emerged from his barge.

There was commotion on the Vulture
As the three barge men,
Hands tied behind their back
Disappeared below deck.
Then a ship cannon blew
The barge to smithereens,
Sinking it into the Hudson,
As if it never existed.

Chris most always wore his
Red Uniform and his British hat
With a black plume
He shouted to Wolf Dog U.S.W.D-14
Who he named, McRat.
"Hurry, McRat, we have work to do!
Let's zoom!
You guard and down a hole I'll scat!"

Washington would never lay eyes
on Arnold again.
Benedict Arnold would become Brigadier
General Under Washington's hated,
King George III.
Now he was on The Vulture.
How fitting, Benedict Arnold was a vulture.
McMole had to act fast!

Whose roof is this anyway?

George Washington's Mount Vernon.
It is very famous because it
was built, it was the only red roof
in the colonies.

Meantime down the hill Christopher flew.
Wolf Dog guarded Mole Hill No. 22
Christopher hopped into Tunnel I-60,
Then under it another tunnel, I-70,
Taking him to an inn
Where the British mole spies
Were sure to be in.
He asked,
"Did you hear the blasts
 From the ship
with the black sails and masts?"

It seems that Arnold was
Planning to capture
Commander Washington
At West Point
And they would now win the colonies,
Always be under the British rule.
But something strange had happened!

Spy McMole fitting in with his red coat,
Heard an alarming tale.
Their human famous counter spy,
John Andre who used the alias,
John Anderson, had been
Apprehended on a country road
By three low-rank U.S. soldiers,
Who guarded this lonely road.

POOR King GEORGE! WOE IS US!
I've got to REMAIN Calm and get up to McRat
KIN ORC

Along came this stranger on his horse.
John Anderson/Andre, of course.
They commanded him to dismount,
In fact, they had to shout, "Dismount."
He was handsome and lean.
Didn't look mean,
But he looked nervous and like he
Had something up his sleeve.

Not up his sleeve, but in his sock!
They asked him to remove his boots.
One sock looked suspect.
Sure enough
Inside this sock some papers fell out.
He was a spy the papers confirmed!
This news was very bad!

They read that Benedict Arnold was
About to capture Commander Washington,
Alexander Hamilton, and Mr. Billy Lee,
Washington's right-hand man,
Who was like Washington's brother.
This would happen at West Point.
This famous fort would now
Belong to King George.
And King George would win the war.
The British moles/spies were very sad.

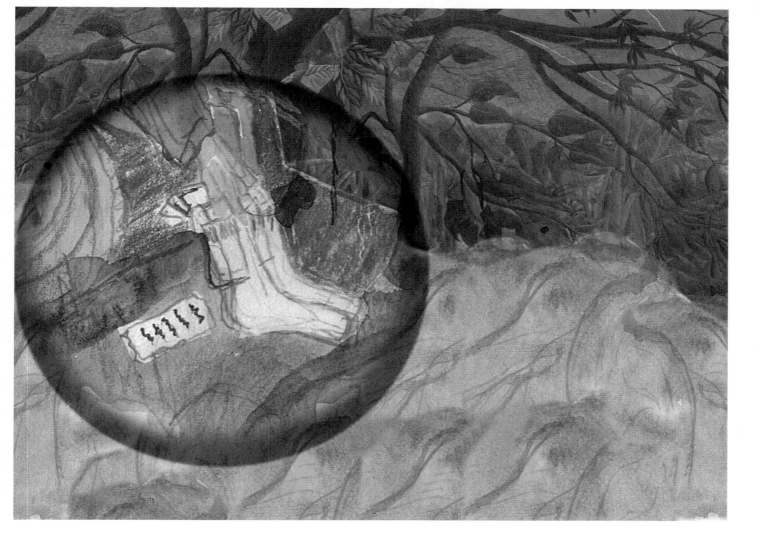

Chapter Two

In McMole's century
No one had a blackberry,
I-phone, or a walkie-talkie.
They depended on a rooster's crow
Or a Franklin clock.

Secretly, Commander Washington
Had spy master, Christopher McMole,
Place wolf dogs 10 miles apart,
Well within their hearing range.
Their military partners trained them
To sound out two long "howls"
 and one short "woof"
For the British ships going North.
Two short "woofs" and two long "howls"
For the British ships going South.
Three "woofs" and three "howls"
for more British ships coming into the harbors
at Manhattan or Long Island.
Wild wolves and the British couldn't figure out
What this was all about!

McMole would keep watch.
With the British moles he would mingle.
At the Manhattan and Long Island harbors
If he saw new British ships coming into port,
He would give the signal.

McMole listened to the scuttlebutt
Coming from the British mole spies
That a turncoat from the Brits
Became a general for the Colonists!
Horatio Gates,
A soldier with sketchy fighting skills,
Wanted to take over the Command
That George Washington had.
His pipe dream was not granted.
No matter what Gates thought.
Washington was the man!
McMole knew!

Commander Washington knew the land
And rode the best horse around, Nelson.
Given him from his friend, Mr. Nelson.
This horse was not afraid of cannon fire,
gun fire, or high fences.
Washington and Mr. Billy Lee were
the best horsemen in the country.
Remember, they were frontiersmen,
Not afraid of the red coats and
their tired way of marching in rows.

The troops respected Washington.
His generals simply wore the Brits down.
Cornwallis
    The Howes
       Clinton
          Gage
             Arnold
Had no chance
They were simply outclassed!

Washington's men were great, and how!
Dealing with them for him
Was a wow!
Just think--
Ethan Alan
  Francis Marion (The Swamp Fox)
   Horatio Gates
    Nathanael Greene
     Alexander Hamilton
      The Green Mountain Boys
      William Heath

Oh, what a relief!

The Red Coats led
By Lord Charles Cornwallis.
Marched in rows, how quaint!
For them, not so keen.
    Samuel Graves
        Thomas Gage
           William Howe
              Richard Howe
                Henry Clinton
                  Guy Carleton
These fellows thought that
The Americans were not in their league.
Cornwallis had a comeupance
That was bigger than big!

Lieutenant Colonel Alexander Hamilton

Washington knew he was right.
Mr. Lee
    Nelson
        Madam Moose
Would ride on a raft at night
With Washington by their side
In the winter cold.
Ice floes and fog all over--everywhere!
Across rivers, the Potomac and the Delaware.

The Swamp Fox

Their raft was always last.
So Washington saw that his troops
Were safely across to the other side.
They crossed at night
Leaving their campfires bright
So the Brits were unaware
That in the early morning
There would be a fight.
The Americans were loose as gooses
And the surprised Brits would be the losers.

Meanwhile,
Traitor, General Arnold, poor guy,
Sailed the Vulture at night
When there was no light
And couldn't figure out
What Washington and his troops were about.
He fought for a year.
And sailed in fear
Because Commander Washington
Was creative, smart, and brave.
He knew the land and had
Better spies.

So off to Canada he fled.
Shortly thereafter,
The better commander, Washington,
Tricked the mighty Cornwallis
That he was going to pick a battle
in Manhattan,
But, no, he was going to put his troops
At Yorktown
And bring the arrogant British General down.

"TWENTY-FOUR WAR SHIPS
THAT'S WHAT WE NEED!"
Ben Franklin sailed to France
to plead.
With his famous charm
No need for alarm.
He got ships that were large
In fact, the Ville de Paris
It had 110 cannons on board.
The Brits were outclassed.
The French shot down their masts.
These 24 ships
Who was in Charge?...

A Frenchman by the name of de Grasse
Captained a fleet of ships
From the West Indies
And blocked Cornwallis
in Yorktown
And the Earl and his men
 Were hemmed in.

De Grasse's fleet were like ducks all in a row
But instead of feathers
They sported cannons.

Author Note

On the next page you will find geese flying in a "V" formation. In Washington's time thousands of geese visited the Chesapeake area every year. For a delightful story about Canadian geese read *Chesapeake* by James A. Michener, chapter, *Voyage Eight: 1822*. My painting of geese, shown here, is "Love in the Cornfield."

Cornwallis was a poor sport,
Failed to turn up at the Brits' surrender.
His troops of 7000 had to walk through
The lines of Americans and the French
And drop their guns.
Humiliated by marching past the
Ones who won.

Cornwallis was cowering in his redoubt,
(A man-made tunnel),
Under his fort.
McMole peeked in and was in disbelief
This tunnel was a mess,
Unlike the moles' tunnels
Which had castles and
Were beautiful to behold.

Cornwallis sent his sword instead
to Washington who said,
"I don't want to touch it."
And the Brit stand-in had to give it
To Washington's second in command

**The Case of
The *Mysterious*
Sword
No one knows where it is**

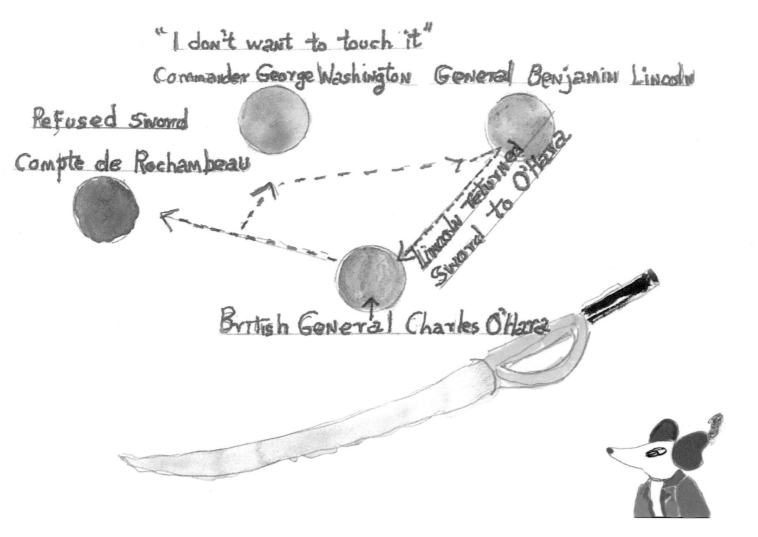

Christopher McMole took a look
and was proud as he could be
of Washington, Mr. Lee, Nelson,
Madam Moose, and, of course the troops.

The HMS Vulture later sailed to France
and became a whaler ship.
Benedict Arnold retired to England
Where he belonged--a traitor
To the new nation that would
Rule the seas for 250
Years or more.

Christopher McMole said to himself,

Commander Washington, a job well done.
Our country is blessed.
No one could have done it
With more courage and finesse!!!

EPILOGUE

The people knew how great Washington was
And they came in droves to visit Mount Vernon
To show him their respect.
Not only to see Washington,
But to see Mr. Billy Lee,
Nelson, the famous war horse,
And to pet Madam Moose!

After the war Washington enjoyed
A short time with his wife, Mr. Lee,
Nelson, and Madam Moose,
To work in his garden
And to become President of the United States.
He helped design the White House and
Washington, DC, with Pierre Charles L'Enfant.

He knew he was destined to be
a great man and wrote many
journals that are in Mount Vernon to this day.
Thank you, Mr. President, who led the
Revolution. You are truly the Father of
Our Country, the United States of America.

Bibliography

Cook, Roy Bird, Virginia Frontier Defense, 1719 - 1795
Vol I1, pp. 119 - 130

Chernow, Ron, Washington A Life The Penquin Press,
New York, 2010

Michener, James A., Chesapeake, Dial iPress
Paperbacks, New York, eBook

Rousseau, Henri, the painting, "Surprised"

Wiley, Samuel T., History of Monongalia County.West Virginia
Preston Publishing Company, Kingwood, W. Va
Chapters VII, VIII

Made in the USA
Las Vegas, NV
07 July 2021

26075256R10055